PRINCEWILL LAGANG

Data-Driven Entrepreneurship: Decisions in the Information Age

First published by PRINCEWILL LAGANG 2023

Copyright © 2023 by Princewill Lagang

All rights reserved. No part of this publication may be reproduced, stored or transmitted in any form or by any means, electronic, mechanical, photocopying, recording, scanning, or otherwise without written permission from the publisher. It is illegal to copy this book, post it to a website, or distribute it by any other means without permission.

Princewill Lagang asserts the moral right to be identified as the author of this work.

First edition

*This book was professionally typeset on Reedsy.
Find out more at reedsy.com*

Contents

1 The Data-Driven Revolution — 1
2 The Foundation of Data Collection — 5
3 Extracting Insights: Data Analysis and Interpretation — 9
4 Predictive Analytics: Shaping the Future — 14
5 Practical Applications of Predictive Analytics — 19
6 Prescriptive Analytics: Guiding Smart Decisions — 24
7 Embracing Data-Driven Excellence — 28
8 Summary — 32

1

The Data-Driven Revolution

In the bustling heart of Silicon Valley, a new breed of entrepreneur was emerging. These individuals were not just visionaries with big ideas; they were data-driven, analytical, and methodical in their approach to building businesses. They weren't relying on gut instincts alone; instead, they were harnessing the power of information to make strategic decisions. This marked the beginning of a new era in entrepreneurship – the Information Age.

1.1 The Evolution of Entrepreneurship

Entrepreneurship has always been about innovation, risk-taking, and seizing opportunities. From the time of the first traders along the Silk Road to the industrial barons of the 19th century, entrepreneurs have shaped the world's economies and societies. Yet, the way entrepreneurs operate has transformed over the years.

Historically, entrepreneurs were often guided by intuition and limited information. They had to rely on their instincts, knowledge, and the advice of a few trusted advisors. The Information Age, however, has ushered in a fundamental shift in how entrepreneurs navigate the business landscape.

1.2 The Data-Driven Advantage

Data-driven entrepreneurship represents a paradigm shift in the way businesses are conceived, developed, and operated. The concept is simple: instead of making critical decisions based solely on intuition or experience, entrepreneurs today are leveraging the vast amounts of data available to them.

Data-driven entrepreneurs:

- Collect and analyze data to understand market trends, consumer behavior, and competitive landscapes.
    - Use data to identify emerging opportunities and potential threats.
    - Optimize their operations and marketing strategies based on quantitative insights.
    - Make well-informed decisions with a higher probability of success.

Data-driven decision-making is not limited to large corporations with vast resources. Startups and small businesses are also embracing this approach, often with remarkable results. The democratization of data and the availability of affordable analytics tools have made it accessible to entrepreneurs of all sizes.

1.3 The Power of Data

Data is more than just numbers and statistics. It's the lifeblood of the modern economy. From the online purchases you make to the steps you take with your fitness tracker, from the posts you like on social media to the weather data that influences your vacation plans, data is everywhere. The ability to collect, process, and interpret this data is a game-changer for entrepreneurs.

Data empowers entrepreneurs in the following ways:

1. Market Understanding: It provides insights into consumer preferences and behavior, allowing entrepreneurs to tailor their products or services accordingly.

2. Risk Mitigation: Data can help identify potential pitfalls and market uncertainties, enabling entrepreneurs to develop contingency plans.

3. Innovation: It fosters innovation by uncovering gaps in the market or areas where existing solutions can be improved.

4. Efficiency: Data-driven automation streamlines business operations, reduces costs, and enhances productivity.

5. Marketing Precision: It allows for highly targeted marketing campaigns, resulting in better returns on investment.

6. Competitive Advantage: Entrepreneurs who harness data effectively gain a significant edge over competitors who do not.

1.4 The Entrepreneur's Dilemma

While the potential benefits of data-driven entrepreneurship are clear, many entrepreneurs face challenges in adopting this approach. It can be daunting to transition from traditional, instinct-based decision-making to a more analytical and data-focused mindset.

The entrepreneur's dilemma lies in finding the right balance between intuition and data. How much should you rely on your gut feeling, and when should you defer to the data? This book will explore these questions and provide guidance on how to navigate this balancing act.

1.5 The Road Ahead

In the chapters that follow, we will delve deep into the world of data-driven entrepreneurship. We will explore the tools and techniques that entrepreneurs can use to collect, analyze, and leverage data. We will discuss real-world case studies of successful data-driven startups and established businesses.

Whether you're an aspiring entrepreneur, a startup founder, or a seasoned business leader, this book will equip you with the knowledge and skills to thrive in the Information Age. Data-driven entrepreneurship is not just a trend; it's the future of business. Are you ready to embrace the revolution?

In the next chapter, we will lay the groundwork for your data-driven journey, exploring the fundamental principles of data collection and analysis. So, fasten your seatbelts, and let's embark on this exciting adventure into the world of data-driven entrepreneurship.

2

The Foundation of Data Collection

In the Information Age, data is the currency of success. It's the raw material from which insights, strategies, and decisions are forged. In this chapter, we'll delve into the foundational aspects of data collection, exploring how to gather the right data and ensure its quality and relevance. Without a solid data collection strategy, your data-driven entrepreneurial journey is likely to be a ship adrift in a sea of information.

2.1 Defining Your Data Needs

The first step in effective data collection is to define what data you need. This involves clarifying your business objectives, understanding your target audience, and identifying the key performance indicators (KPIs) that matter most to your venture. Without a clear purpose, you risk collecting data that may be interesting but ultimately irrelevant to your goals.

Key considerations when defining your data needs:

- Business Goals: What are your short-term and long-term objectives? How can data support these goals?

- Audience Insights: Who are your customers? What do they value? What are their behaviors and preferences?

- KPIs: What metrics are essential for measuring success? Examples include conversion rates, customer retention, and sales figures.

- Competitive Analysis: What data can help you understand your competitors and identify opportunities or threats?

- Operational Efficiency: How can data streamline your business operations and reduce costs?

2.2 Data Sources

Once you've defined your data needs, you must identify the sources from which you'll collect data. Data can come from various channels, and the choice of sources depends on your specific requirements. Common data sources for entrepreneurs include:

1. Internal Data: This includes data generated within your business, such as customer records, sales figures, and website analytics.

2. External Data: External sources, such as industry reports, government data, and market research, can provide valuable context and insights.

3. Customer Feedback: Surveys, reviews, and direct customer feedback can be a goldmine of information about your products and services.

4. Social Media: Social media platforms offer real-time data on consumer sentiment, trends, and competitor activities.

5. Third-Party Data Providers: Many companies offer data services, such as demographic information, market trends, and consumer behavior data.

6. IoT (Internet of Things): If relevant to your business, IoT devices can provide real-time data on product usage and performance.

Choosing the right data sources requires a combination of business acumen and technological knowledge. It's important to ensure that the data you collect is ethical and complies with relevant privacy regulations.

2.3 Data Collection Methods

The methods you employ to gather data will depend on the nature of the data and your objectives. Here are some common data collection methods:

1. Surveys and Questionnaires: These are excellent for collecting structured data from a specific group of respondents.

2. Interviews: In-depth interviews can provide rich qualitative data, particularly useful for understanding customer needs and pain points.

3. Observation: Directly observing user behavior can yield valuable insights, especially in UX (User Experience) research.

4. Web and Social Media Analytics: Tools like Google Analytics and social media insights provide data on website traffic and online engagement.

5. A/B Testing: This method involves comparing two versions of a webpage or product to determine which performs better.

6. APIs (Application Programming Interfaces): Use APIs to gather data from external sources, like social media platforms or financial institutions.

7. Web Scraping: This technique involves extracting data from websites. However, it must be done ethically and within legal boundaries.

2.4 Data Quality and Privacy

The quality of your data is of paramount importance. Poor-quality data can lead to inaccurate insights and flawed decision-making. To ensure data quality, consider the following:

- Accuracy: Data should be free of errors or discrepancies.
   - Completeness: Ensure that data is comprehensive and not missing key information.
   - Consistency: Data should be uniform and not contradict itself.
   - Relevance: Data collected should align with your defined objectives.
   - Timeliness: Real-time data can be crucial, especially in fast-moving markets.

Furthermore, data privacy is a growing concern in the digital age. Collecting, storing, and processing personal data must comply with applicable data protection laws, such as the GDPR in Europe or CCPA in California. Entrepreneurs must be diligent in safeguarding the privacy of their customers' data to build trust and avoid legal repercussions.

2.5 Data Collection Strategy

To bring it all together, you need a comprehensive data collection strategy. This strategy should outline what data you will collect, how you will collect it, and how you will ensure data quality and privacy. It should be a living document, regularly reviewed and updated to stay aligned with your evolving business needs.

Remember that data collection is not a one-time effort; it's an ongoing process. In the next chapter, we'll explore data analysis and the tools available to extract actionable insights from the data you've collected. So, as you embark on your data-driven journey, ensure your data collection foundation is rock-solid.

3

Extracting Insights: Data Analysis and Interpretation

Data collection is just the first step in your data-driven entrepreneurial journey. In this chapter, we dive into the world of data analysis, where raw data is transformed into actionable insights. Understanding how to analyze and interpret data is crucial for making informed decisions that can drive your business forward.

3.1 The Data Analysis Process

Data analysis is not about crunching numbers; it's about uncovering meaningful patterns and insights hidden within your data. The process of data analysis typically involves the following steps:

Step 1: Data Cleaning

Before analysis can begin, you must clean and preprocess the data. This involves removing duplicates, handling missing values, and transforming data into a consistent format. Clean data is essential for accurate analysis.

Step 2: Data Exploration

Exploratory data analysis (EDA) involves visualizing and summarizing data to identify patterns and relationships. Common techniques include histograms, scatter plots, and summary statistics.

Step 3: Hypothesis Testing

Based on your exploratory analysis, you can form hypotheses about your data. These hypotheses help guide more in-depth analysis to test your assumptions and discover significant insights.

Step 4: Data Modeling

Modeling involves creating mathematical or statistical models to predict future trends or relationships. Common methods include regression analysis, time series analysis, and machine learning algorithms.

Step 5: Interpretation and Validation

Once you've completed your analysis, it's crucial to interpret the results in the context of your business goals. You should also validate your findings by checking for statistical significance and practical relevance.

3.2 Tools for Data Analysis

To conduct effective data analysis, you'll need the right tools. The choice of tools depends on the complexity of your analysis and your technical expertise. Here are some commonly used tools:

1. Spreadsheet Software: Excel or Google Sheets is suitable for basic data analysis.

2. Data Analytics Platforms: Tools like Tableau, Power BI, and Google Data Studio offer more advanced visualization and analysis capabilities.

3. Statistical Software: R and Python with libraries like Pandas, NumPy, and Scikit-learn are popular for statistical analysis and machine learning.

4. Database Management Systems (DBMS): For handling and querying large datasets, SQL-based DBMS like MySQL and PostgreSQL are essential.

5. Big Data Tools: In cases of massive datasets, tools like Hadoop and Spark may be necessary.

6. Custom Software: Sometimes, you might need to develop custom software or scripts tailored to your specific data and analysis needs.

The choice of tools will also depend on your budget and the scale of your operations.

3.3 Data Visualization

Data visualization is a vital aspect of data analysis. Well-designed visualizations can make complex data more understandable and help in decision-making. Common types of data visualizations include:

- Bar Charts: Useful for comparing data across categories.
    - Line Charts: Suitable for showing trends over time.
    - Scatter Plots: Display relationships between two variables.
    - Pie Charts: Show the composition of a whole.
    - Heatmaps: Reveal patterns in large datasets.
    - Interactive Dashboards: Combine multiple visualizations for a holistic view of data.

Remember that the choice of visualization depends on the type of data you're working with and the message you want to convey.

3.4 Making Data-Driven Decisions

Data analysis is not just about generating insights; it's about using those insights to make informed decisions. To make data-driven decisions:

- Define Objectives: Clearly state the decision you want to make based on the data analysis.

- Prioritize Insights: Focus on the most relevant and impactful insights.

- Consider Risks: Understand the potential risks and uncertainties associated with your decisions.

- Monitor Outcomes: Implement the decision and continuously monitor its impact. Adjust as necessary.

- Feedback Loop: Use the results of your decision to refine your data collection and analysis processes.

- Communication: Share the insights and decisions with relevant stakeholders in your organization.

3.5 Case Study: Optimizing Ad Campaigns

To illustrate the data analysis process, we'll explore a case study of a startup optimizing its online advertising campaigns. In this example, we'll see how data analysis can help the company improve ad performance, reduce costs, and maximize ROI.

3.6 Next Steps

EXTRACTING INSIGHTS: DATA ANALYSIS AND INTERPRETATION

In the next chapter, we'll dive deeper into advanced data analysis techniques and explore the world of predictive analytics. We'll learn how to use data not just for historical insights but also for forecasting future trends and making proactive decisions.

Data analysis is the bridge between data collection and data-driven decision-making. Mastering this skill is essential for any data-driven entrepreneur. So, let's continue the journey and unlock the full potential of your data.

4

Predictive Analytics: Shaping the Future

Data analysis has given us insights into the past and present, but what if we could peer into the future? In this chapter, we explore the fascinating world of predictive analytics, a powerful tool for data-driven entrepreneurship. By forecasting future trends and outcomes, you can make proactive decisions that set your business on a path to success.

4.1 The Power of Predictive Analytics

Predictive analytics is the practice of using historical data and statistical algorithms to make predictions about future events. In the context of entrepreneurship, it can help you:

- Forecast Sales: Predict future sales trends and revenue, allowing for more accurate financial planning.

- Customer Behavior: Understand how customers are likely to react to changes in products or marketing strategies.

- Resource Allocation: Optimize resource allocation by predicting demand

and supply needs.

- Risk Management: Identify potential risks and threats in advance, enabling better risk mitigation.

- Product Development: Predict market trends and user preferences to guide product development.

4.2 The Predictive Analytics Process

The predictive analytics process involves several key stages:

Step 1: Data Collection

As discussed in previous chapters, data is the foundation of predictive analytics. Ensure you collect relevant and high-quality data.

Step 2: Data Preprocessing

Cleaning and preprocessing data is crucial for predictive analytics, as inaccurate or incomplete data can lead to flawed predictions.

Step 3: Feature Selection

Select the most relevant features (variables) for prediction. Eliminate irrelevant or redundant variables.

Step 4: Model Selection

Choose a suitable predictive model, which can be linear regression, decision trees, neural networks, or other algorithms depending on your data and objectives.

Step 5: Model Training

Train your selected model using historical data. The model learns patterns and relationships from the data.

Step 6: Model Evaluation

Assess the performance of the model using evaluation metrics like Mean Absolute Error (MAE) or Root Mean Squared Error (RMSE).

Step 7: Deployment

Deploy the trained model to make predictions on new, unseen data.

Step 8: Monitoring and Feedback

Continuously monitor the model's performance and retrain it as necessary to maintain accuracy.

4.3 Tools for Predictive Analytics

A variety of tools and libraries can assist in predictive analytics:

1. Python Libraries: Scikit-learn, TensorFlow, and Keras are popular choices for building predictive models.

2. R: R is a language specifically designed for statistical analysis and is well-suited for predictive modeling.

3. Predictive Analytics Software: Software like IBM SPSS and SAS Enterprise Miner provides a user-friendly interface for predictive analytics.

4. Cloud Platforms: Cloud platforms such as AWS, Azure, and Google Cloud

offer machine learning and predictive analytics services.

Selecting the right tool depends on your technical expertise and the complexity of your predictive modeling tasks.

4.4 Case Study: Demand Forecasting

To illustrate predictive analytics in action, let's explore a case study of a retail startup. The company aims to optimize its inventory management by predicting demand for products. By using historical sales data, seasonal patterns, and other factors, the startup can avoid overstocking or understocking, thus reducing costs and improving customer satisfaction.

4.5 Ethical Considerations

Predictive analytics can be a double-edged sword. While it offers great potential, it also raises ethical concerns. Predictive models can unintentionally perpetuate biases present in historical data, leading to unfair outcomes. Entrepreneurs must be mindful of these ethical considerations and take steps to address them in their predictive analytics processes.

4.6 The Future of Predictive Analytics

As technology advances and more data becomes available, the future of predictive analytics is promising. Machine learning and artificial intelligence will continue to play a significant role in predictive modeling, making it even more accurate and accessible for entrepreneurs.

4.7 Next Steps

In the next chapter, we will explore how entrepreneurs can use predictive analytics to make strategic decisions in various aspects of their business, from marketing to finance. We'll delve into practical applications and provide guidance on implementing predictive analytics effectively.

Predictive analytics allows you to be proactive in your decision-making, shaping a better future for your business. So, let's embrace the power of prediction and guide our entrepreneurial journey toward success.

5

Practical Applications of Predictive Analytics

Predictive analytics is a game-changer for data-driven entrepreneurs. In this chapter, we explore how predictive analytics can be applied in various aspects of your business, from marketing and sales to finance and operations. By harnessing the power of prediction, you can make informed decisions that drive success in every facet of your venture.

5.1 Marketing Optimization

Customer Segmentation

Predictive analytics allows you to segment your customer base effectively. By understanding customer behavior and preferences, you can tailor marketing strategies to specific segments, increasing the relevance and impact of your campaigns.

Churn Prediction

Predict when customers are likely to churn (stop using your product or service). Armed with this knowledge, you can implement retention strategies to reduce churn and enhance customer loyalty.

Personalized Recommendations

Leverage predictive algorithms to offer personalized product recommendations to customers. This not only enhances the customer experience but also boosts sales.

5.2 Sales Forecasting

Predictive analytics enables accurate sales forecasting, helping you plan inventory, staffing, and marketing efforts effectively. You can anticipate seasonal trends, market fluctuations, and even the impact of external events on sales.

5.3 Financial Management

Budgeting and Expense Forecasting

Forecasting revenue and expenses is essential for financial planning. Predictive analytics can help you create realistic budgets and manage cash flow effectively.

Fraud Detection

Detect unusual financial transactions or fraudulent activities in real-time using predictive models. This is crucial for protecting your business from financial losses.

Credit Risk Assessment

If your business offers credit to customers, predictive models can assess the creditworthiness of applicants, reducing the risk of bad debt.

5.4 Operations Optimization

Inventory Management

Optimize inventory levels by predicting demand and reducing carrying costs. This prevents overstocking or understocking and ensures efficient operations.

Supply Chain Management

Predictive analytics can help you anticipate disruptions in the supply chain, allowing for contingency planning and risk mitigation.

Maintenance and Repairs

Use predictive models to schedule maintenance and repairs for equipment or assets when they are most likely to fail, saving time and money.

5.5 Human Resources

Recruitment and Talent Acquisition

Predictive analytics can assist in finding the right candidates by assessing resumes and predicting which applicants are most likely to succeed in a particular role.

Employee Turnover

Identify employees at risk of leaving the company before they do. This allows you to implement retention strategies and maintain a stable workforce.

Performance Management

Predictive analytics can help you assess employee performance and identify areas for improvement, leading to better decision-making in promotions, raises, or training.

5.6 Case Study: Marketing Campaign Optimization

In a case study, we'll explore how a startup uses predictive analytics to optimize its marketing campaigns. By analyzing customer data, purchase history, and online behavior, the company tailors its advertising efforts to individual customers. This approach significantly increases campaign efficiency and ROI.

5.7 Challenges and Considerations

While predictive analytics offers immense potential, it comes with challenges, including data privacy, model accuracy, and implementation costs. Entrepreneurs must navigate these obstacles carefully and ensure ethical and responsible use of predictive analytics.

5.8 The Road Ahead

Predictive analytics is a dynamic field, and the possibilities are continually expanding. As technology and data science capabilities evolve, entrepreneurs can expect even more advanced and accessible tools for predictive analytics. Staying current with these developments will be key to maintaining a competitive edge.

5.9 Next Steps

In the next chapter, we'll explore the concept of prescriptive analytics, taking data-driven decision-making to the next level. We'll discover how prescriptive analytics goes beyond predicting outcomes and provides recommendations for action, enabling entrepreneurs to optimize their strategies and operations.

Predictive analytics is a valuable tool for data-driven entrepreneurs, and its applications are limited only by your creativity and the quality of your data. So, let's continue on this journey of data-driven success and unlock the full potential of predictive analytics.

6

Prescriptive Analytics: Guiding Smart Decisions

Predictive analytics offers the power of foresight, but what if you could go a step further and receive actionable recommendations for your next move? In this chapter, we explore the world of prescriptive analytics, where data-driven entrepreneurs are not only predicting outcomes but also being guided toward the best course of action to optimize their strategies and operations.

6.1 The Promise of Prescriptive Analytics

Prescriptive analytics takes data-driven decision-making to the next level. It provides recommendations for the most optimal actions to achieve specific goals. In entrepreneurship, this means that you can leverage data to not only predict future outcomes but also make choices that maximize success.

6.2 Understanding the Components

Prescriptive analytics consists of several essential components:

Data Collection and Analysis

Similar to predictive analytics, prescriptive analytics begins with collecting and analyzing data. This data forms the basis for generating recommendations.

Machine Learning and Algorithms

Prescriptive models utilize advanced machine learning algorithms to process data and provide insights.

Optimization Techniques

Optimization algorithms, such as linear programming and integer programming, are used to find the best solutions to complex business problems.

6.3 Applications in Entrepreneurship

Prescriptive analytics can be applied in various entrepreneurial scenarios:

Pricing Optimization

Determine the optimal pricing strategy that maximizes revenue while considering factors like demand elasticity, competitor pricing, and customer behavior.

Inventory Management

Find the right balance between stock levels and carrying costs by optimizing reorder points and order quantities.

Resource Allocation

Allocate resources efficiently, whether it's funds, personnel, or equipment, to achieve the best return on investment.

Supply Chain Optimization

Make real-time decisions about routing, shipping, and inventory to reduce costs and improve delivery times.

Marketing Campaigns

Optimize marketing budgets and strategies by identifying the most effective channels and message targeting for different customer segments.

6.4 Case Study: Dynamic Pricing Strategy

In a case study, we'll explore how an e-commerce startup uses prescriptive analytics to implement a dynamic pricing strategy. By considering market demand, competitor pricing, and inventory levels, the company adjusts its prices in real-time to maximize revenue while maintaining competitiveness.

6.5 Challenges and Considerations

Implementing prescriptive analytics can be complex. It requires the integration of multiple data sources, advanced algorithms, and real-time decision-making. Ethical considerations, such as fairness and transparency in decision recommendations, are also critical.

6.6 Building a Prescriptive Analytics Culture

To successfully integrate prescriptive analytics into your entrepreneurial ventures, it's crucial to foster a data-driven culture. This includes:

- Leadership Support: Ensuring that leadership recognizes the value of prescriptive analytics and actively supports its implementation.

- Data Literacy: Building data literacy among employees so they can understand and trust the recommendations.

- Data Infrastructure: Developing a robust data infrastructure to support real-time data collection and analysis.

- Change Management: Preparing your organization to adapt to the recommendations generated by prescriptive analytics.

6.7 The Future of Prescriptive Analytics

Prescriptive analytics is an evolving field with enormous potential. As artificial intelligence and machine learning technologies advance, entrepreneurs can expect even more advanced and automated prescriptive models to guide their decisions.

6.8 Next Steps

In the final chapter of this book, we'll bring together the concepts of predictive and prescriptive analytics to provide a roadmap for entrepreneurs to fully embrace data-driven decision-making. We'll explore best practices, potential pitfalls, and the critical role of human judgment in harnessing the power of data for business success.

Prescriptive analytics empowers entrepreneurs with actionable recommendations, making it a critical tool for those striving for data-driven excellence. Let's proceed to the final chapter to complete our journey into the world of data-driven entrepreneurship.

7

Embracing Data-Driven Excellence

In the final chapter of our journey into the world of data-driven entrepreneurship, we explore the path to embracing data-driven excellence. We'll examine best practices, potential pitfalls, and the pivotal role of human judgment in harnessing the power of data for business success.

7.1 Best Practices for Data-Driven Entrepreneurship

1. Define Clear Objectives

Begin with well-defined business objectives. Know what you aim to achieve and how data can support these goals.

2. Data Quality Matters

Ensure data quality by collecting, cleaning, and maintaining accurate and up-to-date data. Poor data quality can lead to flawed insights and decisions.

3. Invest in Data Skills

Foster data literacy in your organization. Equip employees with the skills to understand and leverage data effectively.

4. Build a Robust Data Infrastructure

Invest in the necessary data infrastructure, including data storage, processing, and analysis tools. Cloud solutions can provide scalability and flexibility.

5. Ethics and Privacy

Understand and comply with data privacy laws and ethical considerations. Protect customer data and ensure transparency in data use.

6. Experimentation and A/B Testing

Foster a culture of experimentation. Use A/B testing to assess the impact of changes and improvements.

7. Combine Predictive and Prescriptive Analytics

Leverage both predictive and prescriptive analytics for comprehensive decision support. Predictive analytics provides insights, while prescriptive analytics guides actions.

8. Human Judgment

Recognize that data is a valuable tool, but human judgment is equally crucial. Data can inform decisions, but experienced judgment helps validate and contextualize data insights.

7.2 Potential Pitfalls to Avoid

1. Overreliance on Data

While data is invaluable, avoid the trap of blindly following data-driven recommendations. Always consider the broader context and use your business acumen and expertise.

2. Misinterpretation

Data can be complex and subject to misinterpretation. Ensure that those making decisions based on data are well-equipped to understand and draw accurate conclusions from it.

3. Data Silos

Data silos, where information is compartmentalized and not shared across the organization, hinder collaboration and the ability to make holistic decisions.

4. Neglecting Data Security

Data breaches can be detrimental to both your business and your customers. Implement strong data security measures to safeguard sensitive information.

5. Lack of Feedback Loops

Successful data-driven decision-making involves continuous feedback and iteration. Ensure that decisions are evaluated and refined over time.

7.3 The Role of Leadership

Leadership is pivotal in creating a data-driven culture. As a data-driven entrepreneur, you can set the tone for your organization:

- Lead by Example: Show a commitment to data-driven decision-making and use data to inform your own choices.

- Foster Learning: Encourage a culture of continuous learning and improvement, especially when it comes to data and analytics.

- Promote Collaboration: Break down data silos and facilitate cross-functional collaboration to share data insights and drive collective decision-making.

7.4 The Future of Data-Driven Entrepreneurship

The future holds exciting prospects for data-driven entrepreneurship:

- Artificial Intelligence: AI will play an increasing role in data analysis, automation, and decision-making.

- Blockchain: This technology offers secure and transparent data storage, which could further enhance data integrity.

- Data Ethics: Ethical considerations will continue to be paramount in data-driven decision-making.

- Data Regulation: Data privacy laws and regulations are likely to evolve, shaping how businesses handle data.

7.5 Your Journey Ahead

As you embark on your data-driven entrepreneurial journey, remember that data is a tool, not a destination. It empowers you to make informed decisions, but your vision, leadership, and judgment are what will truly guide your business to success.

Data-driven excellence is an ongoing endeavor. It requires dedication, a willingness to learn, and the flexibility to adapt. Embrace this journey, and your business will thrive in the Information Age.

8

Summary

Chapter 1: The Data-Driven Revolution
 - Introduces data-driven entrepreneurship in the Information Age.
 - Discusses the historical evolution of entrepreneurship and the shift towards data-driven decision-making.
 - Explores the advantages of data-driven entrepreneurship and its accessibility to businesses of all sizes.

Chapter 2: The Foundation of Data Collection

- Discusses the importance of defining data needs and sources.
 - Covers data collection methods and considerations for data quality and privacy.
 - Emphasizes the need for a comprehensive data collection strategy as the foundation of data-driven decision-making.

Chapter 3: Extracting Insights: Data Analysis and Interpretation

- Explores the data analysis process, including data cleaning, exploration, hypothesis testing, and modeling.
 - Introduces various tools for data analysis and the significance of data

visualization.
 - Includes a case study on optimizing marketing campaigns through data analysis.

Chapter 4: Predictive Analytics: Shaping the Future

- Introduces predictive analytics and its applications in forecasting future trends.
 - Explores the predictive analytics process and the tools used for predictive modeling.
 - Includes a case study on demand forecasting and discusses the ethical considerations and the future of predictive analytics.

Chapter 5: Practical Applications of Predictive Analytics

- Demonstrates how predictive analytics can be applied in various aspects of entrepreneurship, including marketing, sales, finance, operations, and human resources.
 - Includes a case study on marketing campaign optimization and discusses the challenges and considerations related to using predictive analytics.

Chapter 6: Prescriptive Analytics: Guiding Smart Decisions

- Introduces prescriptive analytics and its role in providing recommendations for optimal actions.
 - Discusses the components of prescriptive analytics and its applications in entrepreneurship, including pricing optimization, inventory management, and supply chain optimization.
 - Includes a case study on implementing a dynamic pricing strategy and examines the challenges and considerations associated with prescriptive analytics.

Chapter 7: Embracing Data-Driven Excellence

- Outlines best practices for data-driven entrepreneurship, including defining objectives, ensuring data quality, and fostering data skills.

- Highlights potential pitfalls to avoid, such as overreliance on data and neglecting data security.

- Discusses the role of leadership in creating a data-driven culture and looks at the future of data-driven entrepreneurship.

The book emphasizes the importance of data in the modern entrepreneurial landscape and guides readers through the process of collecting, analyzing, and leveraging data for informed decision-making. It provides practical insights, case studies, and recommendations for building a data-driven culture within an organization.

www.ingramcontent.com/pod-product-compliance
Lightning Source LLC
LaVergne TN
LVHW010441070526
838199LV00066B/6124